HEARTY ASIAN CONGEE RECIPES

CONGEE CREATIONS

L TRAN

About Author

L Tran, an esteemed cookbook author weaving the tapestry of flavors from her rich Asian heritage into the global culinary landscape, stands as a beacon of cultural celebration and gastronomic innovation.

Born into a family where the kitchen was the heart of the home, Tran's earliest memories are imbued with the aromas of spices, the sizzle of stir-fries, and the artistry of traditional Asian cooking techniques. Raised in a household where food was synonymous with love and connection, she developed an unwavering passion for the culinary arts from a tender age.

Guided by her family's culinary legacy and nurtured by generations-old recipes passed down with care, Tran embarked on a journey to explore the intricate nuances of Asian cuisine. Her quest led her through bustling markets, serene tea plantations, and intimate kitchens, where she absorbed the wisdom of elders and honed her skills in the art of flavor harmonization.

Tran's unwavering dedication to honoring her roots while embracing innovation has solidified her place as a trailblazer in the culinary sphere. With each recipe and endeavor, she continues to bridge cultures and inspire others to embark on their own flavorful journeys through the captivating realm of Asian cuisine.

History of Asian Congee

Asian congee, a comforting rice porridge, has a long and varied history across the continent, reflecting its deep cultural significance and versatility. Originating in ancient China, congee has been a staple food for over two millennia, dating back to the Zhou Dynasty (1046–256 BCE). In its earliest forms, it was a simple dish made by boiling rice in water, often consumed by the elderly, sick, or as a humble meal for the poor. Its ease of preparation and digestibility made it a favored dish for those in need of nourishment.

Over time, congee spread to neighboring regions and adapted to local tastes and ingredients. In Korea, it became known as "juk," and was commonly enjoyed as a nutritious meal during illness or for breakfast. Korean congee often features ingredients like seafood or vegetables, showcasing its versatility. In Japan, congee, or "okayu," also serves as a soothing dish, especially for those recovering from illness. Japanese congee is typically simpler, with a milder flavor and often eaten with pickles or seasoned with soy sauce.

In Southeast Asia, congee evolved into a variety of regional dishes, each reflecting local flavors and customs. In Vietnam, for instance, "cháo" is a common breakfast item or comforting dish during illness, frequently garnished with herbs, meat, and vegetables. Similarly, in Thailand, congee, known as "jok," is enjoyed with a variety of toppings, including preserved eggs, minced pork, and fresh cilantro.

Throughout its history, Asian congee has maintained its role as a versatile, nourishing, and comforting dish. Its adaptation across different cultures highlights its fundamental appeal as a simple yet satisfying meal that continues to be cherished in many Asian cuisines today.

Table of Content

Table of Content

Bai Zhou

Prep Time	Cooking Time	Serving Size
10 minutes	1 hour	4 servings

Ingredients:

- 1 cup jasmine rice or short-grain rice
- 10 cups water (or more, depending on the desired consistency)
- 1/4 teaspoon salt (optional)
- Optional toppings: pickled vegetables, salted eggs, century eggs, stir-fried peanuts, scallions, or sesame oil.

Instructions:

To prepare the rice, start by rinsing it thoroughly under cold water until the water runs clear. This step is important as it removes excess starch, ensuring a smoother texture in the porridge.

Next, cook the rice by placing it in a large pot along with 10 cups of water. Bring the mixture to a boil over medium-high heat. Once it reaches a boil, reduce the heat to low and let it simmer uncovered. Be sure to stir occasionally to prevent the rice from sticking to the bottom of the pot. Simmer the rice for about 1 to 1.5 hours, depending on how thick and smooth you prefer the porridge. If needed, add more water to achieve the desired consistency. The rice should break down, resulting in a creamy texture.

If you wish to season the porridge, you can add 1/4 teaspoon of salt, or adjust to taste. Stir the salt in well.

Finally, ladle the Bai Zhou into bowls and serve hot. You can enjoy it plain or enhance the dish with toppings such as pickled vegetables, salted eggs, century eggs, stir-fried peanuts, scallions, or a drizzle of sesame oil. Enjoy!

Notes:

- *Adjust the water amount based on how thick or thin you prefer the porridge. For a thicker porridge, reduce the water by 1 to 2 cups; for a thinner porridge, add more water.*
- *If you like a creamier texture, you can blend part of the porridge with a hand blender.*

Century Egg & Pork Congee

Prep Time	**Cooking Time**	**Serving Size**
20 minutes	1.5 hour	4 servings

Ingredients:

- 1 cup jasmine rice or short-grain rice
- 8 cups water (or chicken broth for more flavor)
- 200 grams (7 oz) ground pork
- 2 century eggs, peeled and diced
- 1 tablespoon soy sauce
- 1 tablespoon Shaoxing wine (optional)
- 1/4 teaspoon white pepper
- 1/4 teaspoon salt, or to taste
- 1 thumb-sized piece of ginger, julienned
- 2 green onions, finely chopped (for garnish)
- Sesame oil, for drizzling (optional)
- Fried shallots (optional)

Instructions:

Begin by rinsing the rice thoroughly under cold water until the water runs clear. This step helps to remove excess starch, ensuring the porridge will have a smoother texture.

To cook the rice, combine the rinsed rice and 8 cups of water or chicken broth in a large pot. Bring the mixture to a boil over medium-high heat. Once it reaches a boil, reduce the heat to low and let it simmer uncovered, stirring occasionally to prevent the rice from sticking to the bottom of the pot. Simmer for about an hour, or until the rice has broken down and the congee has reached a creamy consistency. If needed, add more water or broth to achieve your desired thickness.

While the congee is simmering, prepare the pork by mixing the ground pork with soy sauce, Shaoxing wine (if using), white pepper, and salt. Allow the pork to marinate for 10-15 minutes.

Once the congee has reached your preferred consistency, add the marinated ground pork to the pot. Stir well to break up the pork, and cook it for about 5-7 minutes, or until the pork is fully cooked.

Next, stir in the diced century eggs and julienned ginger. Let the congee simmer for another 5 minutes to allow the flavors to blend.

Finally, taste the congee and adjust the seasoning with more salt or white pepper if needed. Ladle the congee into bowls and garnish with chopped green onions, a drizzle of sesame oil, and fried shallots, if desired, before serving.

This Century Egg and Pork Congee is warming, comforting, and packed with umami flavors. Enjoy!

Fish Congee

Prep Time	**Cooking Time**	**Serving Size**
20 minutes	1 hour	4 servings

Ingredients:

- 1 cup jasmine rice or short-grain rice
- 8 cups water (or chicken broth for more flavor)
- 300 grams (10 oz) fresh white fish fillets (like cod, tilapia, or sea bass), thinly sliced
- 1 tablespoon soy sauce
- 1 tablespoon Shaoxing wine (optional)
- 1/4 teaspoon white pepper
- 1/4 teaspoon salt, or to taste
- 1 thumb-sized piece of ginger, julienned
- 2 green onions, finely chopped (for garnish)
- 2 tablespoons sesame oil (optional)
- Fried shallots (optional)

Instructions:

Start by rinsing the rice under cold water until the water runs clear. This step removes excess starch, helping to create a smoother congee.

To cook the rice, place the rinsed rice in a large pot with 8 cups of water or chicken broth. Bring the mixture to a boil over medium-high heat. Once boiling, reduce the heat to low and allow the rice to simmer uncovered. Stir occasionally to prevent the rice from sticking to the bottom of the pot. Let it simmer for about 1 hour, or until the rice has broken down and the congee reaches a creamy consistency. If you prefer a thinner porridge, add more water as needed.

While the congee is cooking, prepare the fish by marinating the sliced fish fillets with soy sauce, Shaoxing wine (if using), white pepper, and a pinch of salt. Allow the fish to marinate for 15 minutes.

When the congee reaches your desired thickness, stir in the julienned ginger. Next, add the marinated fish slices to the congee. Let the fish cook gently in the hot congee for about 3-5 minutes, or until the fish turns opaque and is fully cooked.

Finally, taste the congee and adjust the seasoning with additional salt or white pepper, if needed. Ladle the fish congee into bowls, and garnish with chopped green onions, a drizzle of sesame oil, and fried shallots, if desired. Serve hot and enjoy!

Notes:

- *Fish cooks quickly in the hot congee, so be careful not to overcook it to keep the texture tender.*

Chicken Congee

Prep Time
20 minutes

Cooking Time
1 hour

Serving Size
4 servings

Ingredients:

- 1 cup jasmine rice or short-grain rice
- 8 cups water (or chicken broth for more flavor)
- 300 grams (10 oz) boneless, skinless chicken breasts or thighs
- 1 tablespoon soy sauce
- 1 tablespoon Shaoxing wine (optional)
- 1 thumb-sized piece of ginger, julienned
- 2 green onions, finely chopped (for garnish)
- 1/4 teaspoon white pepper
- 1/2 teaspoon salt, or to taste
- 1 tablespoon sesame oil (optional)
- Fried shallots (optional)

Instructions:

Begin by rinsing the rice under cold water until the water runs clear. This step helps remove excess starch, resulting in a smoother texture for the congee.

To cook the rice, place the rinsed rice into a large pot along with 8 cups of water or chicken broth. Bring the mixture to a boil over medium-high heat. Once boiling, lower the heat to a simmer and cook uncovered, stirring occasionally to prevent the rice from sticking. Allow the rice to simmer for about 1 hour, or until it has broken down and the congee reaches a creamy consistency. You can add more water or broth if needed to achieve your preferred thickness.

While the congee is cooking, prepare the chicken by marinating it with soy sauce, Shaoxing wine (if using), a pinch of salt, and white pepper. Let it marinate for 15 minutes. After marinating, you can either boil the chicken separately for 10-15 minutes and shred it into thin pieces, or add it directly to the congee to cook.

Once the chicken is ready, stir the shredded chicken into the congee and let it simmer for an additional 5 minutes to blend the flavors.

To finish, stir in the julienned ginger and taste the congee. Adjust the seasoning with additional salt or white pepper if needed. Ladle the chicken congee into bowls and garnish with chopped green onions, a drizzle of sesame oil, and fried shallots if desired. Serve hot and enjoy!

Duck Congee

Prep Time	**Cooking Time**	**Serving Size**
20 minutes	2 hours	4 servings

Ingredients:

- 1 cup jasmine rice or short-grain rice
- 8 cups water (or chicken broth for extra flavor)
- 2 duck legs (or 300 grams duck breast, skin-on if possible)
- 1 tablespoon soy sauce
- 1 tablespoon Shaoxing wine (optional)
- 1 thumb-sized piece of ginger, julienned
- 2 green onions, finely chopped (for garnish)
- 1/2 teaspoon white pepper
- 1/2 teaspoon salt, or to taste
- 1 tablespoon sesame oil (optional)
- 1 tablespoon hoisin sauce (optional)
- Fried shallots or crispy garlic (optional)
- Fresh cilantro (optional)

Instructions:

Start by preparing the rice. Rinse the rice under cold water until the water runs clear, removing excess starch. This step ensures a smoother texture in the congee.

To cook the duck, place the duck legs or breast in a large pot with 8 cups of water or chicken broth, along with a few slices of ginger. Bring the mixture to a boil, then reduce the heat to low and simmer for about 45 minutes to 1 hour, or until the duck is tender and fully cooked. Once done, remove the duck from the pot and allow it to cool slightly. Shred the meat into thin pieces, discarding the bones and skin if you're using duck legs. Set the shredded duck aside for later.

Now, cook the rice. In the same pot with the duck broth, add the rinsed rice and bring it to a boil. Lower the heat to a simmer and cook for about 1 hour, stirring occasionally to prevent the rice from sticking. As the rice cooks, it will break down and create a creamy texture. If the congee becomes too thick, feel free to add more water or broth to achieve your desired consistency.

Once the congee reaches the desired texture, stir in the shredded duck meat and let it simmer for an additional 5 minutes to blend the flavors.

To season the congee, add soy sauce, Shaoxing wine (if using), white pepper, and salt to taste. Stir well to combine all the seasonings.

Finally, ladle the duck congee into bowls and garnish with julienned ginger, chopped green onions, a drizzle of sesame oil, and crispy garlic or fried shallots, if desired. You can also enhance the flavor with a dollop of hoisin sauce or some fresh cilantro. Serve and enjoy!

Beef Congee

Prep Time	Cooking Time	Serving Size
25 minutes	1 hour	4 servings

Ingredients:

- 1 cup jasmine rice or short-grain rice
- 8 cups water (or beef broth for richer flavor)
- 250 grams (8 oz) ground beef (flank steak, sirloin, or tenderloin)
- 1 tablespoon soy sauce
- 1 tablespoon Shaoxing wine (optional)
- 1/4 teaspoon white pepper
- 1/4 teaspoon salt, or to taste
- 2 green onions, finely chopped (for garnish)
- 1 teaspoon crushed white pepper (optional)
- 1 tablespoon sesame oil (optional)

Instructions:

Start by rinsing the rice under cold water until the water runs clear, which will help remove excess starch and result in a smoother congee.

To cook the rice, combine the rinsed rice and 8 cups of water or beef broth in a large pot. Bring the mixture to a boil over medium-high heat, then reduce the heat to low and simmer uncovered. Stir occasionally to prevent the rice from sticking to the bottom of the pot. Let it simmer for about 1 hour, or until the rice has broken down into a creamy texture. If the congee becomes too thick, add more water or broth as needed.

While the congee is cooking, prepare the beef by marinating the ground beef with soy sauce, Shaoxing wine (if using), white pepper, and a pinch of salt. Let the beef marinate for 15-20 minutes.

Once the congee reaches your desired consistency, stir in the marinated beef and cook for 3-5 minutes, just until the beef is tender and cooked through. Be careful not to overcook the beef to keep it tender. Taste and adjust the seasoning with more salt or white pepper, if necessary.

To serve, ladle the beef congee into bowls and garnish with chopped green onions, crushed pepper, and a drizzle of sesame oil if desired. Enjoy your hearty and flavorful beef congee!

Abalone Congee

Prep Time	Cooking Time	Serving Size
20 minutes	1 hour	4 servings

Ingredients:

- 1 cup jasmine rice or short-grain rice
- 8 cups water (or chicken broth for more flavor)
- 4 small fresh abalones (or 1 can of abalone, sliced)
- 1 medium carrot, diced
- 1 thumb-sized piece of ginger, julienned
- 1 tablespoon soy sauce
- 1/2 teaspoon salt, or to taste
- 1/4 teaspoon white pepper
- 2 green onions, finely chopped (for garnish)
- 1 tablespoon sesame oil (optional)

Instructions:

Start by rinsing the rice under cold water until the water runs clear. This removes excess starch, which helps create a smoother texture for the congee.

Next, prepare the abalone. If you are using fresh abalone, clean it thoroughly and slice it thinly. If using canned abalone, slice it into thin pieces and reserve the liquid from the can for extra flavor.

For cooking the rice, combine the rinsed rice with 8 cups of water or broth in a large pot. Bring the mixture to a boil over medium-high heat. Once it reaches a boil, reduce the heat to low and let it simmer uncovered, stirring occasionally to prevent sticking. Allow the rice to cook for about 1 hour until it breaks down and the congee becomes creamy. If the congee thickens too much, you can add more water or broth to achieve the consistency you prefer.

About 20 minutes into the cooking process, add the diced carrots. Let them soften and cook alongside the rice as it continues to simmer.

Once the congee has reached your desired texture and the carrots are tender, stir in the sliced abalone. If you're using canned abalone, include the reserved liquid for added flavor. Allow the abalone to cook gently for 5-10 minutes, but be careful not to overcook it, as this can make it tough.

To finish, season the congee by adding julienned ginger, soy sauce, salt, and white pepper. Stir well and adjust the seasoning to taste.

When serving, ladle the abalone congee into bowls and garnish with chopped green onions and drizzle of sesame oil for an extra burst of flavor. Enjoy!

Peanut Congee

Prep Time	Cooking Time	Serving Size
2 hours	1.5 hours	4 servings

Ingredients:

- 1 cup jasmine rice or short-grain rice
- 8 cups water (or chicken/vegetable broth for extra flavor)
- 1 cup raw peanuts (with or without skin)
- 1/2 teaspoon salt, or to taste
- 1/4 teaspoon white pepper (optional)
- 2 green onions, finely chopped (for garnish)
- 2 youtiao (Chinese fried dough sticks), sliced into bite-sized pieces

Instructions:

Begin by rinsing the rice under cold water until the water runs clear. This step removes excess starch, which helps achieve a smoother texture in the congee.

If you'd like a softer texture for the peanuts, you can soak them in water for about 2 to 3 hours or overnight. This step is optional but enhances the tenderness of the peanuts.

Next, cook the rice and peanuts. In a large pot, combine the rinsed rice, soaked peanuts (if using), and 8 cups of water or broth. Bring the mixture to a boil over medium-high heat. Once boiling, reduce the heat to low and simmer uncovered for about 1 to 1.5 hours. Stir occasionally to prevent the rice from sticking to the bottom of the pot.

Continue simmering until the rice breaks down and the congee reaches a creamy consistency. By this time, the peanuts should also become tender. If the congee becomes too thick, add more water to reach your preferred consistency.

Once the congee is ready, season it with salt and white pepper to taste. Stir well to incorporate the flavors.

To serve, ladle the peanut congee into bowls. Garnish with chopped green onions for added freshness. You can also enjoy the congee with crispy youtiao slices on the side or placed directly on top for extra texture. Enjoy!

Mushroom Congee

Prep Time	**Cooking Time**	**Serving Size**
20 minutes	1 hour	4 servings

Ingredients:

- 1 cup jasmine rice or short-grain rice
- 8 cups water (or vegetable/ chicken broth for more flavor)
- 200 grams (7 oz) mushrooms (shiitake, button, or a mix), sliced
- 1 tablespoon soy sauce (for sautéing)
- 1 tablespoon cooking oil
- 1/4 teaspoon salt, or to taste
- 1/4 teaspoon white pepper (optional)
- 1 thumb-sized piece of ginger, julienned
- 2 green onions, thinly sliced (for garnish)
- 1 teaspoon sesame oil (optional)

Instructions:

To begin, rinse the rice under cold water until the water runs clear. This helps remove excess starch, ensuring a smoother texture for the congee once it's cooked.

In a large pot, combine the rinsed rice with 8 cups of water or broth and bring it to a boil over medium-high heat. Once it reaches a boil, lower the heat to a simmer and cook uncovered, stirring occasionally to prevent the rice from sticking. Allow the rice to cook for about an hour, or until it breaks down and the congee develops a creamy consistency. If the congee becomes too thick, add more water or broth to adjust the consistency to your liking.

While the congee is simmering, heat 1 tablespoon of oil in a pan over medium heat. Add the sliced mushrooms and cook for 3-5 minutes, allowing them to soften and release their moisture. Drizzle 1 tablespoon of soy sauce over the mushrooms and stir to coat them evenly. Continue cooking for another 1-2 minutes until the soy sauce is fully absorbed, then remove the pan from the heat and set the mushrooms aside.

When the congee has reached your desired texture, stir in the julienned ginger, along with salt and white pepper to taste. Adjust the seasoning as needed.

To serve, ladle the congee into bowls and top each bowl with the sautéed mushrooms. For extra flavor, garnish with sliced green onions and a drizzle of sesame oil, if desired. Enjoy your comforting bowl of congee!

Dried Scallop Congee

Prep Time
1 hours

Cooking Time
1 hour

Serving Size
4 servings

Ingredients:

- 1 cup jasmine rice or short-grain rice
- 8 cups water (or chicken broth for more flavor)
- 6-8 dried scallops (soaked in water for 1 hour)
- 2 honey dates (or dried red dates), soaked and sliced
- 1/4 teaspoon salt, or to taste
- 1/4 teaspoon white pepper (optional)
- 1 thumb-sized piece of ginger, julienned
- 2 green onions, finely chopped (for garnish)
- 1 tablespoon sesame oil (optional)

Instructions:

Begin by rinsing the rice under cold water until the water runs clear. This step removes excess starch, which helps achieve a smoother texture for the congee.

Next, soak the dried scallops in warm water for 1-2 hours until they soften. Reserve the soaking water to add extra flavor to the congee. Once the scallops are softened, shred them into small pieces using your fingers.

In a large pot, combine the rinsed rice, 8 cups of water or broth, and the reserved scallop soaking water. Bring the mixture to a boil over medium-high heat. Once boiling, reduce the heat to low and let it simmer uncovered, stirring occasionally to prevent the rice from sticking. Cook the rice for about an hour, or until it breaks down and the congee has a creamy consistency. If the congee becomes too thick, add more water or broth as needed.

About 20 minutes before the congee is done, add the shredded dried scallops and honey dates. Allow them to simmer with the congee for the remaining cooking time, letting the flavors meld together.

When the congee has reached your desired consistency, stir in julienned ginger, salt, and white pepper (if using). Adjust the seasoning to taste.

To serve, ladle the dried scallop congee into bowls and garnish with sliced honey dates and chopped green onions if desired. For an extra touch of richness, drizzle with sesame oil. Enjoy your flavorful and comforting bowl of congee!

Notes:

- *If you prefer a sweeter touch, you can add more honey dates or serve them on the side for a unique contrast.*
- *The dried scallops provide a natural umami flavor, so adjust salt carefully to keep the dish balanced.*

Cháo Gà

Prep Time
25 minutes

Cooking Time
1.5 hours

Serving Size
4 servings

Ingredients:

- 1 cup jasmine rice or short-grain rice
- 8 cups chicken broth (or water for a lighter version)
- 2 chicken thighs or breasts, boneless and skinless
- 1 thumb-sized piece of ginger, sliced
- 2 green onions, chopped (white parts for cooking, green parts for garnish)
- 1 tablespoon fish sauce (optional)
- 1/2 teaspoon salt, or to taste
- 1/4 teaspoon white pepper (optional)
- 1 tablespoon cooking oil
- Fresh cilantro (for garnish)
- Fried shallots (optional, for garnish)
- Sliced chili peppers (optional, for garnish)
- Lime wedges (optional, for serving)

Instructions:

To start, rinse the rice under cold water until the water runs clear to remove excess starch.

In a large pot, bring 8 cups of chicken broth (or water) to a boil. Add the chicken thighs or breasts along with sliced ginger. Reduce the heat and let it simmer for 20-30 minutes, or until the chicken is cooked through and tender. Once done, remove the chicken from the pot, shred it into bite-sized pieces, and set it aside. Discard the ginger slices.

Using the same pot with the chicken broth, add the rinsed rice. Bring it back to a boil, then reduce the heat to low. Simmer uncovered, stirring occasionally to prevent the rice from sticking to the bottom, for about 1 hour or until the rice breaks down and the congee reaches a creamy consistency. If needed, add more water or broth to achieve your desired thickness.

Stir the shredded chicken back into the congee and let it simmer for another 5-10 minutes to allow the flavors to meld. Adjust the seasoning with fish sauce, salt, and white pepper to taste.

For the garnish, heat 1 tablespoon of cooking oil in a small pan over medium heat. Add the white parts of the green onions and sauté until fragrant. Stir this mixture into the congee.

To serve, ladle the Cháo Gà into bowls. Garnish with chopped green onions, fresh cilantro, fried shallots, and sliced chili peppers if desired. Serve with lime wedges on the side for a splash of tanginess. Enjoy your comforting bowl of Cháo Gà!

Cháo Vịt

Prep Time	Cooking Time	Serving Size
25 minutes	1.5 hours	4 servings

Ingredients:

- 1 cup jasmine rice or short-grain rice
- 8 cups chicken or duck broth (or water for a lighter version)
- 2 duck legs or thighs (bone-in)
- 1 thumb-sized piece of ginger, sliced
- 1 onion, quartered
- 2 cloves garlic, minced
- 1 tablespoon soy sauce
- 1 tablespoon fish sauce (optional)
- 1/2 teaspoon salt, or to taste
- 1/4 teaspoon white pepper (optional)
- 2 green onions, chopped (white parts for cooking, green parts for garnish)
- 1 tablespoon cooking oil
- Fresh cilantro (for garnish)
- Fried shallots (optional, for garnish)
- Sliced chili peppers (optional, for garnish)
- Lime wedges (optional, for serving)

Instructions:

Begin by rinsing the rice under cold water until the water runs clear to remove excess starch. This step ensures a smoother texture in the congee.

In a large pot, bring 8 cups of chicken or duck broth (or water) to a boil. Add the duck legs or thighs along with sliced ginger and quartered onion. Reduce the heat and let it simmer for 30-40 minutes, or until the duck is cooked through and tender. Once done, remove the duck from the pot, discard the onion and ginger, and shred the duck meat into bite-sized pieces. Set it aside.

Using the same pot with the broth, add the rinsed rice. Bring it back to a boil, then reduce the heat to low. Simmer uncovered, stirring occasionally to prevent the rice from sticking to the bottom of the pot, for about 1 hour or until the rice breaks down and the congee reaches a creamy consistency. If needed, add more water or broth to achieve your desired thickness.

To prepare the aromatics, heat 1 tablespoon of cooking oil in a small pan over medium heat. Add minced garlic and cook until fragrant, then stir this mixture into the congee.

Next, stir the shredded duck meat back into the congee. Season with soy sauce, fish sauce (if using), salt, and white pepper. Let the congee simmer for another 5-10 minutes to allow the flavors to meld.

Ladle the Cháo Vịt into bowls and garnish with chopped green onions, fresh cilantro, fried shallots, and sliced chili peppers if desired. Serve with lime wedges on the side for a splash of tanginess. Enjoy your flavorful Cháo Vịt!

Cháo Lòng

Prep Time
30 minutes

Cooking Time
1.5 hour

Serving Size
4 servings

Ingredients:

- 1 cup jasmine rice or short-grain rice
- 8 cups chicken or pork broth (or water for a lighter version)
- 200 grams (7 oz) pork liver, thinly sliced
- 200 grams (7 oz) pork heart, thinly sliced
- 200 grams (7 oz) pork stomach, cleaned and sliced
- 1 thumb-sized piece of ginger, sliced
- 2 cloves garlic, minced
- 1 tablespoon soy sauce
- 1 tablespoon fish sauce (optional)
- 1/2 teaspoon salt, or to taste
- 1/4 teaspoon white pepper (optional)
- 2 green onions, chopped (white parts for cooking, green parts for garnish)
- 1 tablespoon cooking oil
- Fresh cilantro (for garnish)
- Fried shallots (optional, for garnish)
- Sliced chili peppers (optional, for garnish)
- Lime wedges (optional, for serving)

Instructions:

To begin, rinse the rice under cold water until the water runs clear. This step removes excess starch, contributing to a smoother texture in the congee.

Next, prepare the offal. Bring a small pot of water to a boil and blanch the pork liver, heart, and stomach separately for 2-3 minutes to remove impurities. Drain them and rinse under cold water, then slice into thin, bite-sized pieces.

In a large pot, bring 8 cups of chicken or pork broth (or water) to a boil. Add the rinsed rice and ginger slices. Reduce the heat to low and simmer uncovered, stirring occasionally, for about 1 hour, or until the rice has broken down and the congee reaches a creamy consistency. Add more water or broth as needed to achieve your desired thickness.

While the congee cooks, prepare the aromatics by heating 1 tablespoon of cooking oil in a small pan over medium heat. Add minced garlic and cook until fragrant, then stir this mixture into the congee.

Add the sliced pork liver, heart, and stomach to the congee. Continue to simmer for another 10-15 minutes, or until the offal is cooked through and tender. Season with soy sauce, fish sauce (if using), salt, and white pepper, adjusting the seasoning to taste.

Ladle the Cháo Lòng into bowls and garnish with chopped green onions, fresh cilantro, fried shallots, and sliced chili peppers if desired. Serve with lime wedges on the side for a splash of tanginess. Enjoy your Cháo Lòng!

Cháo Tôm

Prep Time
25 minutes

Cooking Time
1 hour

Serving Size
4 servings

Ingredients:

- 1 cup jasmine rice or short-grain rice
- 8 cups chicken or seafood broth (or water for a lighter version)
- 200 grams (7 oz) shrimp, peeled and deveined
- 1 thumb-sized piece of ginger, sliced
- 2 cloves garlic, minced
- 1 tablespoon soy sauce
- 1 tablespoon fish sauce (optional)
- 1/2 teaspoon salt, or to taste
- 1/4 teaspoon white pepper (optional)
- 2 green onions, chopped (white parts for cooking, green parts for garnish)
- 1 tablespoon cooking oil
- Fresh cilantro (for garnish)
- Fried shallots (optional, for garnish)
- Sliced chili peppers (optional, for garnish)
- Lime wedges (optional, for serving)

Instructions:

To begin, rinse the rice under cold water until the water runs clear. This step helps remove excess starch and ensures a smoother texture in the congee.

In a large pot, bring 8 cups of chicken or seafood broth (or water) to a boil. Add the rinsed rice and sliced ginger, then reduce the heat to low. Simmer uncovered, stirring occasionally, for about 1 hour, or until the rice breaks down and the congee reaches a creamy consistency. Adjust the thickness by adding more water or broth if necessary.

While the rice is cooking, prepare the shrimp. Heat 1 tablespoon of cooking oil in a pan over medium heat. Add minced garlic and cook until fragrant. Then, add the shrimp and cook until they turn pink and are cooked through, about 2-3 minutes. Season with soy sauce and fish sauce (if using), then remove from heat and set aside.

Once the congee has reached the desired consistency, stir in the cooked shrimp. Let it simmer for an additional 5 minutes to allow the flavors to meld. Season with salt and white pepper to taste.

Ladle the Cháo Tôm into bowls and garnish with chopped green onions, fresh cilantro, fried shallots, and sliced chili peppers if desired. Serve with lime wedges on the side for a splash of tanginess. Enjoy your Cháo Tôm!

Cháo Cá

Prep Time
20 minutes

Cooking Time
1 hour

Serving Size
4 servings

Ingredients:

- 1 cup jasmine rice or short-grain rice
- 8 cups chicken or fish broth (or water for a lighter version)
- 300 grams (10 oz) white fish fillets (such as cod, tilapia, or catfish), skinless and boneless
- 1 thumb-sized piece of ginger, sliced
- 2 cloves garlic, minced
- 1 tablespoon fish sauce (or soy sauce)
- 1/2 teaspoon salt, or to taste
- 1/4 teaspoon white pepper (optional)
- 2 green onions, chopped (white parts for cooking, green parts for garnish)
- 1 tablespoon cooking oil
- Fresh cilantro (for garnish)
- Fried shallots (optional, for garnish)
- Sliced chili peppers (optional, for garnish)
- Lime wedges (optional, for serving)

Instructions:

Start by rinsing the rice under cold water until the water runs clear. This process helps remove excess starch, which contributes to a smoother texture in the congee.

Next, in a large pot, bring 8 cups of chicken or fish broth (or water) to a boil. Add the rinsed rice and sliced ginger, then reduce the heat to low. Let the mixture simmer uncovered, stirring occasionally, for about 1 hour. This will allow the rice to break down and the congee to achieve a creamy consistency. If the congee becomes too thick, add more water or broth as needed.

While the rice is cooking, prepare the fish. Heat 1 tablespoon of cooking oil in a pan over medium heat. Add minced garlic and cook until fragrant. Then, add the fish fillets and cook until they are opaque and cooked through, about 3-5 minutes per side, depending on their thickness. Remove the fish from the pan, flake it into bite-sized pieces, and set aside.

Once the congee has reached your desired consistency, stir in the flaked fish. Let it simmer for an additional 5 minutes to allow the flavors to meld. Season with fish sauce, salt, and white pepper to taste.

Ladle the Cháo Cá into bowls and garnish with chopped green onions, fresh cilantro, fried shallots, and sliced chili peppers if desired. Serve with lime wedges on the side for a splash of tanginess. Enjoy your Cháo Cá!

Cháo Hải Sản

Prep Time
25 minutes

Cooking Time
1 hour

Serving Size
4 servings

Ingredients:

- 1 cup jasmine rice or short-grain rice
- 8 cups seafood or chicken broth (or water for a lighter version)
- 150 grams (5 oz) shrimp, peeled and deveined
- 150 grams (5 oz) squid, cleaned and sliced into rings
- 150 grams (5 oz) fish fillets (such as cod or tilapia), skinless and boneless, cut into bite-sized pieces
- 1 thumb-sized piece of ginger, sliced
- 2 cloves garlic, minced
- 1 tablespoon fish sauce (or soy sauce)
- 1/2 teaspoon salt, or to taste
- 1/4 teaspoon white pepper (optional)
- 2 green onions, chopped (white parts for cooking, green parts for garnish)
- 1 tablespoon cooking oil
- Fresh cilantro (for garnish)
- Fried shallots (optional, for garnish)
- Sliced chili peppers (optional, for garnish)
- Lime wedges (optional, for serving)

Instructions:

Begin by rinsing the rice under cold water until the water runs clear. This step removes excess starch and ensures a smoother texture in the congee.

In a large pot, bring 8 cups of seafood or chicken broth (or water) to a boil. Add the rinsed rice and sliced ginger, then reduce the heat to low. Simmer uncovered, stirring occasionally, for about 1 hour, until the rice breaks down and the congee achieves a creamy consistency. If the congee becomes too thick, add more water or broth as needed.

While the rice is cooking, prepare the seafood. Heat 1 tablespoon of cooking oil in a pan over medium heat. Add minced garlic and cook until fragrant. Then, add the shrimp, squid, and fish fillets to the pan. Cook until the shrimp turn pink, the squid rings become opaque, and the fish is cooked through, which should take about 3-5 minutes. Remove the seafood from the pan and set it aside.

Once the congee has reached your desired consistency, stir in the cooked seafood. Simmer for an additional 5-10 minutes to allow the flavors to meld. Season with fish sauce, salt, and white pepper to taste.

Ladle the Cháo Hải Sản into bowls and garnish with chopped green onions, fresh cilantro, fried shallots, and sliced chili peppers if desired. Serve with lime wedges on the side for a splash of tanginess. Enjoy your Cháo Hải Sản!

Zosui

Prep Time	**Cooking Time**	**Serving Size**
25 minutes	35 minutes	4 servings

Ingredients:

- 2 cups cooked rice (preferably leftover rice, but freshly cooked rice works too)
- 4 cups chicken or vegetable broth
- 200 grams (7 oz) chicken breast or thigh, thinly sliced (or you can use leftover chicken)
- 1 thumb-sized piece of ginger, sliced
- 2 cloves garlic, minced
- 1 tablespoon soy sauce
- 1 tablespoon mirin (optional)
- 1 tablespoon sake (optional)
- 1/2 teaspoon salt, or to taste
- 1/4 teaspoon white pepper (optional)
- 1/2 cup mushrooms (shiitake, enoki, or button mushrooms), sliced
- 1/2 cup julienne carrot
- 2 green onions, chopped (white parts for cooking, green parts for garnish)
- 1 tablespoon cooking oil
- Fresh cilantro or parsley (for garnish, optional)
- Pickled vegetables or umeboshi (Japanese pickled plums, optional, for serving)

Instructions:

To prepare the broth, start by bringing 4 cups of chicken or vegetable broth to a simmer in a large pot.

In a separate pan, heat 1 tablespoon of cooking oil over medium heat. Add minced garlic and sliced ginger, sautéing until fragrant. Then, add the thinly sliced chicken to the pan and cook until it is no longer pink and is fully cooked through. Season with soy sauce, mirin, and sake (if using), then remove from heat and set aside.

Next, add the cooked rice to the simmering broth, stirring well. Allow it to cook for about 5-10 minutes until the rice is heated through and the flavors meld together. Add the sliced mushrooms and julienne carrots to the pot and cook for an additional 5 minutes, or until they are tender.

Stir the cooked chicken into the pot and let it simmer for a few more minutes to ensure all the flavors are well combined. Season with salt and white pepper to taste.

Ladle the Zosui into bowls and garnish with chopped green onions and fresh cilantro or parsley if desired. Serve with pickled vegetables or umeboshi on the side for added flavor and texture. Enjoy your Zosui!

Tamago Okayu

Prep Time	**Cooking Time**	**Serving Size**
15 minutes	1 hour	4 servings

Ingredients:

- 1 cup jasmine rice or short-grain rice
- 6 cups chicken or vegetable broth (or water for a lighter version)
- 4 large eggs
- 1 thumb-sized piece of ginger, sliced (optional)
- 2 green onions, chopped (white parts for cooking, green parts for garnish)
- 1 tablespoon soy sauce
- 1/2 teaspoon salt, or to taste
- 1/4 teaspoon white pepper (optional)
- 1 sheet nori (seaweed), cut into thin strips (for garnish)
- 1 tablespoon cooking oil (optional, for sautéing)

Instructions:

To prepare the Tamago Okayu, start by rinsing the rice under cold water until the water runs clear. This removes excess starch and helps create a smoother texture in the congee.

In a large pot, bring 6 cups of chicken or vegetable broth (or water) to a boil. Add the rinsed rice and sliced ginger if using. Reduce the heat to low and simmer uncovered, stirring occasionally. Cook for about 45 minutes to 1 hour, or until the rice has broken down and the porridge reaches a creamy consistency. If the porridge becomes too thick, add more water or broth as needed to achieve your desired thickness.

While the rice is cooking, bring a small pot of water to a gentle simmer. Carefully crack each egg into the simmering water and poach for about 2-3 minutes, or until the whites are set but the yolks remain runny. Use a slotted spoon to remove the eggs and set them aside.

Once the congee has reached the desired consistency, stir in the soy sauce, salt, and white pepper. Adjust the seasoning to taste.

Ladle the Tamago Okayu into bowls and top each bowl with a poached egg. Garnish with chopped green onions and strips of nori. For extra flavor, you can optionally sauté the white parts of the green onions in a little oil until fragrant before adding them to the porridge. Enjoy your meal!

Notes:

- *If you prefer a firmer egg, cook it a bit longer, but keep in mind that the traditional Tamago Okayu has a runny yolk.*

Nanakusa Gayu

Prep Time	**Cooking Time**	**Serving Size**
20 minutes	1 hour	4 servings

Ingredients:

- 1 cup short-grain rice or jasmine rice
- 7 cups water (or a light dashi broth for extra flavor)
- 1/2 teaspoon salt (or to taste)
- 1/4 teaspoon white pepper (optional)
- 1/4 cup water dropwort (or spinach)
- 1/4 cup shepherd's purse (or arugula)
- 1/4 cup cudweed (or mizuna)
- 1/4 cup chickweed (or parsley)
- 1/4 cup nipplewort (or watercress)
- 1/4 cup turnip greens
- 1/4 cup radish greens
- 1 small turnip, peeled and thinly sliced (optional)
- 1 small daikon radish, peeled and thinly sliced (optional)
- 2 green onions, finely chopped (for garnish)

Instructions:

To prepare Nanakusa-Gayu (Seven-Herb Porridge), start by rinsing the rice under cold water until the water runs clear, which helps remove excess starch and ensures a smooth porridge texture.

In a large pot, bring 7 cups of water or light dashi broth to a boil. Add the rinsed rice and stir well. Lower the heat to a simmer and cook uncovered, stirring occasionally, for about 45 minutes to 1 hour, or until the rice breaks down and the porridge becomes creamy. If needed, add more water to achieve your preferred consistency.

While the rice is cooking, thoroughly wash the herbs. If using larger greens like turnip or radish greens, chop them into bite-sized pieces. If including turnip or daikon, thinly slice them for adding later.

Once the rice has reached a creamy consistency, add the sliced turnip, daikon (if using), and the prepared herbs. Cook for an additional 2-3 minutes, until the greens are wilted and tender.

Stir in the salt and white pepper, adjusting the seasoning to your taste.

Serve the Nanakusa-Gayu in bowls, and optionally garnish with finely chopped green onions. Enjoy the refreshing, nourishing dish!

Sweet Potato Congee

Prep Time
20 minutes

Cooking Time
1 hour

Serving Size
4 servings

Ingredients:

- 1 cup jasmine rice or short-grain rice
- 7 cups water (or chicken/vegetable broth for extra flavor)
- 2 medium sweet potatoes, peeled and cut into 1-inch cubes
- 1/2 teaspoon salt (or to taste)
- 1 tablespoon sugar (optional, if you like a sweeter version)
- 1/4 teaspoon white pepper (optional)
- 1 tablespoon cooking oil (optional, for a richer taste)
- Sliced green onions (for garnish)

Instructions:

To make sweet potato congee, begin by rinsing the rice under cold water until the water runs clear, removing excess starch for a smoother texture.

In a large pot, bring 7 cups of water or broth to a boil. Add the rinsed rice and reduce the heat to low. Simmer uncovered for 45 minutes to 1 hour, stirring occasionally to prevent sticking. The congee will thicken as the rice breaks down.

After about 30 minutes, when the congee has started to thicken, add the sweet potato cubes. Continue cooking for another 15-20 minutes, until the sweet potatoes are tender and easily pierced with a fork.

Once the sweet potatoes are done, season the congee with salt and white pepper to taste. If you prefer a sweeter version, stir in 1 tablespoon of sugar. For added richness, you can mix in 1 tablespoon of cooking oil.

Ladle the congee into bowls and garnish with sliced green onions for a fresh, colorful touch. Enjoy!

Dakjuk

Prep Time	**Cooking Time**	**Serving Size**
20 minutes	1.5 hours	4 servings

Ingredients:

- 1 cup short-grain rice (or sushi rice)
- 6 cups water or chicken broth
- 2 boneless, skinless chicken breasts (or thighs for richer flavor)
- 1 tablespoon sesame oil
- 4 cloves garlic, minced
- 1 tablespoon soy sauce (optional)
- 1/2 teaspoon salt, or to taste
- 1/4 teaspoon white pepper, or to taste
- 2 green onions, chopped (for garnish)
- Toasted sesame seeds (for garnish)

Instructions:

To prepare Dakjuk (Korean chicken porridge), begin by rinsing the rice under cold water until the water runs clear, removing excess starch for a smoother texture.

In a large pot, bring 6 cups of water or chicken broth to a boil. Add the chicken breasts and cook for 15-20 minutes over medium heat until the chicken is fully cooked. Remove the chicken from the pot, let it cool slightly, then shred it with two forks and reserve the broth, set aside.

Using the same pot, heat 1 tablespoon of sesame oil over medium heat. Add the rinsed rice and sauté for 2-3 minutes, coating the rice with sesame oil to enhance its flavor.

Next, pour the reserved chicken broth back into the pot with the rice. Add minced garlic and bring the mixture to a boil. Lower the heat and let it simmer uncovered for 45 minutes to 1 hour, stirring occasionally, until the rice breaks down and the congee becomes creamy.

Once the congee reaches the desired consistency, stir in the shredded chicken. Season with soy sauce, salt, and white pepper to taste. Simmer for an additional 5 minutes to allow the flavors to meld together.

Ladle the Dakjuk into bowls and garnish with chopped green onions and toasted sesame seeds for added flavor and texture.

Dakjuk is a wonderfully hearty and soothing dish that's both filling and light, making it ideal for a simple meal, especially when you crave something warm and comforting. Enjoy!

Notes:

- *If you prefer a thinner congee, add more water or broth while cooking.*
- *Dakjuk can also be made with chicken thighs or drumsticks for a richer taste.*

Beef Juk

Prep Time
20 minutes

Cooking Time
1 hour

Serving Size
4 servings

Ingredients:

- 1 cup short-grain rice (or sushi rice)
- 200g (7 oz) beef (sirloin, chuck, or brisket), finely sliced or ground
- 6 cups water or beef broth
- 1 tablespoon sesame oil
- 2 cloves garlic, minced
- 2 tablespoons soy sauce (adjust to taste)
- 1/2 teaspoon salt (adjust to taste)
- 1/4 teaspoon white pepper (optional)
- 2 green onions, finely chopped (for garnish)
- Toasted sesame seeds (for garnish)

Instructions:

To prepare Beef Juk (Korean beef congee), start by rinsing the rice under cold water until the water runs clear, removing excess starch to ensure a smooth texture.

In a large pot, heat 1 tablespoon of sesame oil over medium heat. Add minced garlic and sauté until fragrant, about 1 minute. Add the sliced or ground beef, stir-frying for 3-5 minutes until it's browned and cooked through. Stir in 1 tablespoon of soy sauce for extra flavor.

Add the rinsed rice to the pot with the beef, stirring well to coat the rice with the sesame oil and beef juices. Cook for 2-3 minutes until the rice turns slightly translucent.

Next, pour in 6 cups of water or beef broth and bring the mixture to a boil. Reduce the heat to low, simmering uncovered for 45 minutes to 1 hour, stirring occasionally until the rice breaks down and the congee reaches a creamy consistency. Add more water or broth if needed to adjust the texture.

Season the congee with the remaining soy sauce, salt, and white pepper to taste. Let it cook for another 5 minutes to blend the flavors.

Serve the Beef Juk in bowls, garnishing with chopped green onions and toasted sesame seeds for added flavor and texture.

Yachae Juk

Prep Time	Cooking Time	Serving Size
25 minutes	1 hour	4 servings

Ingredients:

- 1 cup short-grain rice (or sushi rice)
- 7 cups water or vegetable broth
- 1 medium carrot, finely diced
- 1 small zucchini, finely diced
- 1/2 cup spinach, chopped
- 1/2 cup shiitake mushrooms, thinly sliced
- 1 tablespoon sesame oil
- 2 cloves garlic, minced
- 2 tablespoons soy sauce (adjust to taste)
- 1/2 teaspoon salt (adjust to taste)
- 1/4 teaspoon white pepper (optional)
- 2 green onions, chopped (for garnish)
- Toasted sesame seeds (for garnish)

Instructions:

To prepare Yachae Juk (Korean vegetable congee), start by rinsing the rice under cold water until the water runs clear, removing excess starch to achieve a smooth texture.

In a large pot, heat 1 tablespoon of sesame oil over medium heat. Add minced garlic and sauté for about 1 minute until fragrant. Stir in the rinsed rice, cooking for 2-3 minutes, and stirring frequently to coat the rice in sesame oil and garlic.

Next, add diced carrots, zucchini, mushrooms, and spinach to the pot, cooking for an additional 2-3 minutes while mixing the vegetables with the rice.

Pour in 7 cups of water or vegetable broth and bring the mixture to a boil. Reduce the heat to low and let it simmer uncovered for 45 minutes to 1 hour, stirring occasionally until the rice breaks down and the congee reaches a creamy consistency.

Once the desired texture is achieved, season the congee with soy sauce, salt, and white pepper to taste. Let it simmer for an additional 5 minutes to meld the flavors.

Serve the Yachae Juk in bowls, garnishing with chopped green onions and toasted sesame seeds for an extra touch of flavor and texture. Enjoy your Yachae Juk!

Jeonbokjuk

Prep Time
25 minutes

Cooking Time
1 hour

Serving Size
4 servings

Ingredients:

- 1 cup short-grain rice
- 6 cups water or chicken/seafood broth
- 4-6 fresh abalones (or 1 cup canned abalone, drained)
- 1 tablespoon sesame oil
- 2 cloves garlic, minced
- 1 tablespoon soy sauce (adjust to taste)
- 1/2 teaspoon salt (or to taste)
- 1/4 teaspoon white pepper (optional)
- 2 green onions, chopped (for garnish)
- Toasted sesame seeds (for garnish)
- 1 tablespoon chopped fresh ginger (optional, for added flavor)

Instructions:

To prepare Jeonbokjuk (abalone porridge), start by washing the rice under cold water until the water runs clear. This removes excess starch and ensures a smooth texture in the porridge. If using fresh abalone, clean them thoroughly under cold running water, remove the meat from the shells, discard the intestines, and slice the meat thinly. For canned abalone, simply drain and slice.

In a large pot, bring 6 cups of water or chicken/seafood broth to a boil. Add the rinsed rice, then reduce the heat to low. Simmer uncovered for about 45 minutes to 1 hour, stirring occasionally, until the rice breaks down and the congee reaches a creamy consistency.

While the rice is cooking, heat 1 tablespoon of sesame oil in a separate pan over medium heat. Add the minced garlic (and ginger, if using) and sauté until fragrant, about 1 minute. Next, add the sliced abalone to the pan and stir-fry briefly until just cooked through, about 2-3 minutes. Season with a splash of soy sauce, and adjust the seasoning to taste.

Once the rice has become creamy, stir the sautéed abalone into the pot of congee. Continue to simmer for an additional 5-10 minutes to allow the flavors to meld. Season the porridge with additional soy sauce, salt, and white pepper to taste.

Ladle the Jeonbokjuk into bowls and garnish with chopped green onions and toasted sesame seeds for added flavor and texture. Enjoy!

Notes:

- *Adjust the amount of broth or water depending on your desired consistency; more liquid for a thinner porridge and less for a thicker one.*
- *For a richer flavor, use seafood broth instead of water.*

Kimchi Juk

Prep Time
20 minutes

Cooking Time
1 hour

Serving Size
2 servings

Ingredients:

For the Porridge:
- 1 cup short-grain rice
- 6 cups chicken or vegetable broth
- 1 cup kimchi, chopped (use kimchi with plenty of juice)
- 1/2 pound fresh octopus, cleaned and cut into bite-sized pieces
- 2 tablespoons vegetable oil
- 1 onion, finely chopped
- 4 cloves garlic, minced
- 1 thumb-sized piece of ginger, minced
- 2 tablespoons gochujang (Korean red chili paste)
- 2 tablespoons soy sauce (adjust to taste)
- 1 tablespoon sesame oil
- 1 teaspoon salt (adjust to taste)
- 1/2 teaspoon ground black pepper

For Garnish:
- Sliced green onions
- Chopped fresh cilantro (optional)
- Sesame seeds
- Sliced red chili (optional)
- Pickled radish (optional)

Instructions:

To make Kimchi Juk with Octopus, start by rinsing the rice under cold water until it runs clear to remove excess starch.

In a large pot, heat vegetable oil over medium heat. Add chopped onion, minced garlic, and ginger, and sauté until softened and fragrant, about 3-4 minutes.

Add the octopus pieces and cook until they turn opaque, about 3-4 minutes. Remove the octopus from the pot and set it aside.

In the same pot, add the rinsed rice and stir to coat it with the oil and aromatics. Pour in chicken or vegetable broth and bring to a boil. Reduce heat to low and simmer, uncovered, stirring occasionally, until the rice breaks down and the porridge becomes thick and creamy, about 30-40 minutes.

Stir in chopped kimchi and its juice, gochujang, soy sauce, sesame oil, salt, and black pepper. Continue to simmer for another 10-15 minutes to allow the flavors to meld together.

Return the cooked octopus to the pot and stir to combine. Heat through for an additional 5 minutes.

Ladle the Kimchi Juk with Octopus into bowls. Garnish with sliced green onions, sesame seeds, chopped cilantro (if using), and sliced red chili (if desired). Serve with pickled radish on the side if you like.

This dish combines the tangy, spicy flavor of kimchi with the tender, savory octopus, making for a comforting and satisfying meal. Enjoy!

Hobakjuk

Prep Time	**Cooking Time**	**Serving Size**
1 hour	1.5 hour	4 servings

Ingredients:

- 1 small Korean pumpkin (kabocha) or about 2 pounds (unpeeled weight)
- 1/2 cup glutinous rice, soaked in water for at least an hour
- 1/2 teaspoon salt
- 1 tablespoon brown sugar (adjust to taste or exclude)
- 1/4 cup red or white beans (soaked and boiled, optional)
- 1 tablespoon black sesame seeds (optional, for garnish)

Rice Cake Balls:
- 1/2 cup sweet rice flour
- 1/4 teaspoon fine sea salt
- 2 teaspoons sugar
- 4 tablespoons hot water

Instructions:

To prepare Hobakjuk (Korean pumpkin porridge), start by cutting the pumpkin into quadrants. Remove the seeds and stringy bits using a knife or spoon, then place the pumpkin pieces in a large pot. Add enough water to cover about one-third of the pumpkin—approximately 6 cups. Cover the pot and boil over medium-high heat for about 25 minutes, or until the pumpkin is fork-tender. Once cooked, remove the water, transfer the pumpkin to a bowl, and let it cool.

When the pumpkin is cool enough to handle, peel off the skin and discard it. Chop the pumpkin flesh into smaller chunks.

Next, prepare the rice. In a blender, grind the soaked glutinous rice with 1 cup of water until as fine as possible. Pour the ground glutinous rice into the pot with the prepared pumpkin, and add 3 cups of water. Cook over medium heat, stirring and mashing the pumpkin chunks until the rice starts to turn translucent and the porridge thickens. Adjust the consistency by adding more water if needed. Cover the pot, reduce the heat to low, and continue to simmer, stirring occasionally, for about 20 minutes. Stir in the salt, sugar, and cooked red beans (if using), and cook for an additional 3-4 minutes.

If you'd like to make optional rice cake balls, mix rice powder, sugar, and salt in a bowl. Stir in 4 tablespoons of boiling hot water with a spoon. When the mixture is cool enough to handle, knead by hand until a dough forms. Shape the dough into 3/4-inch thick cylinders, cut them into 3/4-inch pieces, and roll each piece into a small ball. Boil water in a small pot, add the rice cake balls, and cook until they float to the surface. Use a strainer to scoop them out and transfer them to a bowl of cold water to cool. Drain before adding them to the porridge.

Ladle the Hobakjuk into bowls, garnish with black sesame seeds if desired, and top with the optional rice cake balls. Enjoy!

Patjuk

Prep Time	**Cooking Time**	**Serving Size**
30 minutes	1.5 hours	4 servings

Ingredients:

For the Red Bean Porridge:
- 1 cup adzuki beans
- 6 cups water (for cooking the beans)
- 1/2 cup sweet rice flour (for thickening, optional)
- 1 tablespoon sesame oil
- 2-3 tablespoons sugar (adjust to taste)
- 1/4 teaspoon salt (adjust to taste)

For the Rice Cake Balls:
- 1/2 cup sweet rice flour (or glutinous rice flour)
- 2 tablespoons sugar
- 1/4 teaspoon salt
- 4 tablespoons boiling water

Instructions:

To prepare Patjuk (Korean red bean porridge), start by rinsing the adzuki beans under cold water. Place them in a large pot with 6 cups of water, and bring to a boil. Once boiling, reduce the heat and let the beans simmer for about 30 minutes, or until they are tender. Drain the beans and, if desired, remove the skins to achieve a smoother texture.

In the same pot, return the cooked beans and add 4 cups of fresh water. Simmer over medium heat until the beans are very soft and begin to break down, which should take about 15-20 minutes. Use a potato masher or spoon to mash the beans to your preferred consistency, whether smooth or slightly chunky.

For a thicker porridge, mix 1/2 cup of sweet rice flour with a little water to form a slurry. Stir this into the pot and continue to simmer, stirring constantly, until the porridge thickens, about 5 minutes. Stir in the sesame oil, sugar, and salt to taste, adjusting the sweetness and seasoning as needed.

To prepare the rice cake balls, mix 1/2 cup of sweet rice flour, 2 tablespoons of sugar, and 1/4 teaspoon of salt in a bowl. Stir in 4 tablespoons of boiling water until the mixture forms a dough. When the dough is cool enough to handle, knead it briefly and shape into small balls, about 1/2 inch in diameter. Boil water in a small pot, add the rice cake balls, and cook until they float to the surface, about 3-5 minutes. Remove with a slotted spoon and transfer to a bowl of cold water to cool, then drain.

Ladle the Patjuk into bowls and garnish with the rice cake balls on top. This comforting dish pairs the rich flavor of red beans with the chewy texture of rice cake balls, making it perfect for a warming winter meal or a special occasion. Enjoy!

Bubur Ayam

Prep Time
30 minutes

Cooking Time
1 hour

Serving Size
4 servings

Ingredients:

For the Congee:
- 1 cup jasmine rice (or short-grain rice)
- 6 cups chicken broth (or water)
- 1 boneless, skinless chicken breast (or thigh), cooked and shredded
- 2 cloves garlic, minced
- 1 tablespoon ginger, minced
- 1 tablespoon soy sauce
- 1 teaspoon sesame oil
- 1 teaspoon salt (adjust to taste)
- 1/2 teaspoon white pepper (optional)

For Garnishes:
- Fried shallots (store-bought or homemade)
- Sliced green onions
- Boiled Egg
- Fried Soy Beans
- Shrimp Crackers (Kerupuk)
- Sambal or chili sauce (optional)

Instructions:

To prepare Bubur Ayam, start by rinsing the rice under cold water until the water runs clear, which helps remove excess starch and ensures a smoother texture.

In a large pot, bring 6 cups of chicken broth to a boil. Add the rinsed rice, then reduce the heat to low. Simmer uncovered, stirring occasionally, for about 45 minutes to 1 hour, or until the rice breaks down and the congee achieves a creamy texture. If the congee becomes too thick, adjust the consistency by adding more broth or water as needed.

While the rice is cooking, heat 1 teaspoon of sesame oil in a small pan over medium heat. Add minced garlic and ginger, and sauté until fragrant, which should take about 1 minute.

Stir in the soy sauce to the pot of congee, then stir in the garlic and ginger mixture along with salt and white pepper. Allow the congee to simmer for an additional 5-10 minutes to let the flavors meld.

Prepare your garnishes while the congee is simmering. Slice green onions, cilantro, cucumber, and tomato. If using, prepare the fried shallots and pickled vegetables.

To serve, ladle the congee into bowls and top with shredded chicken, fried shallots, sliced green onions, halved boiled egg, fried soy beans, and shrimp crackers. For those who enjoy a bit of spice, serve with sambal or chili sauce on the side.

Bubur Ayam is a versatile and comforting dish, customizable with your favorite toppings and sides. It's perfect for a warming meal and can be adjusted to suit your taste preferences. Enjoy!

Notes:

- *Adjust the amount of broth or water depending on your desired consistency; more liquid for a thinner porridge and less for a thicker one.*

Bubur Manado

Prep Time	**Cooking Time**	**Serving Size**
30 minutes	1 hour	4 servings

Ingredients:

For the Porridge:
- 1 cup rice (preferably jasmine or short-grain)
- 5 cups water or chicken broth
- 1 cup pumpkin, diced
- 1 cup sweet corn kernels (fresh or frozen)
- 1 cup green beans, cut into 1-inch pieces
- 1 large potato, diced
- 1 carrot, diced
- 1/2 cup cassava (optional), peeled and diced
- 1 teaspoon turmeric powder
- 1 teaspoon ginger, minced
- 2 cloves garlic, minced
- 1 lemongrass stalk, smashed
- 2 kaffir lime leaves, torn
- 1-2 teaspoons salt (to taste)
- 1/2 teaspoon ground black pepper (optional)

For Garnishes:
- Fried shallots
- Sliced green onions
- Fresh cilantro leaves
- Sliced red chili (optional)
- Sambal (optional)

Instructions:

To prepare Bubur Manado, begin by rinsing the rice under cold water until the water runs clear, which removes excess starch and ensures a smoother porridge texture.

In a large pot, bring 5 cups of water or chicken broth to a boil. Add the rinsed rice, turmeric powder, ginger, garlic, lemongrass, and kaffir lime leaves. Reduce the heat to low and let it simmer, stirring occasionally, for about 20 minutes.

Once the rice has started to break down, add the diced pumpkin, sweet corn, green beans, potato, carrot, and cassava (if using) to the pot. Continue to simmer, stirring occasionally, until the vegetables are tender and the porridge reaches a creamy consistency, which should take about 30-40 minutes. If the porridge becomes too thick, adjust the consistency by adding more water or broth as needed.

Season the porridge with salt and ground black pepper to taste, and adjust the seasoning as desired.

While the porridge is cooking, prepare the garnishes. Slice the green onions, chop the cilantro, and slice red chili if using.

To serve, ladle the Bubur Manado into bowls and top with fried shallots, sliced green onions, fresh cilantro, and red chili if desired. For those who enjoy a spicy kick, serve with sambal on the side.

Bubur Manado is a hearty and flavorful porridge, filled with a variety of vegetables and enhanced by aromatic spices. It's perfect for a comforting meal. Enjoy!

Bubur Kacang Hijau

Prep Time
2 hours

Cooking Time
1 hour

Serving Size
4 servings

Ingredients:

- 1 cup mung beans (green beans), soaked for 1-2 hours or overnight
- 4 cups water
- 1 cup coconut milk (full-fat or light)
- 1-2 tablespoons palm sugar or brown sugar (adjust to taste)
- 1/2 teaspoon salt (adjust to taste)
- 1-2 pandan leaves (optional, tied into a knot for flavor)
- 1-2 tablespoons rice flour (optional, mixed with a little water to make a slurry, for thickening)

Instructions:

To prepare Bubur Kacang Hijau, start by draining the soaked mung beans and rinsing them under cold water.

In a large pot, combine the rinsed mung beans with 4 cups of water. Bring the mixture to a boil, then reduce the heat to low and simmer uncovered. Stir occasionally, until the beans are tender and starting to break apart, which should take about 30-40 minutes.

Once the mung beans are tender, you can either mash them slightly for a smoother texture or leave them as is for a chunkier consistency. Stir in the coconut milk, palm sugar, salt, and pandan leaves (if using). Continue to simmer for an additional 10-15 minutes to allow the flavors to meld and the porridge to thicken.

If you prefer a thicker porridge, mix 1-2 tablespoons of rice flour with a little water to create a slurry. Stir this into the pot and cook for a few more minutes until the porridge reaches your desired thickness.

To serve, ladle the Bubur Kacang Hijau into bowls. Bubur Kacang Hijau is a versatile and delicious dish that can be enjoyed as a breakfast or a snack. Its creamy texture and sweet flavor make it a comforting choice for any time of the day. Enjoy!

Bubur Lambuk

Prep Time	**Cooking Time**	**Serving Size**
20 minutes	1 hour	4 servings

Ingredients:

- 1 cup jasmine rice (or short-grain rice)
- 6 cups chicken or beef broth
- 200 grams chicken thighs or beef (cut into small pieces, optional)
- 2 tablespoons vegetable oil
- 1 onion, finely chopped
- 4 cloves garlic, minced
- 1 thumb-sized piece of ginger, minced
- 2 stalks lemongrass, smashed
- 2-3 kaffir lime leaves (optional, torn)
- 1 teaspoon ground turmeric
- 1 teaspoon ground cumin
- 1 teaspoon ground coriander
- 1/2 teaspoon ground black pepper
- 2 tablespoons soy sauce or fish sauce (adjust to taste)
- 1 teaspoon salt (adjust to taste)
- 1 tablespoon sugar (optional, to balance flavors)
- 1 cup coconut milk (optional, for creaminess)

For Garnish:
- Fried shallots
- Chopped fresh cilantro
- Sliced red chili (optional)
- Lime wedges

Instructions:

To prepare Bubur Lambuk, start by rinsing the rice under cold water until the water runs clear, which helps remove excess starch.

For the meat (if using), heat vegetable oil in a large pot over medium heat. Add the chopped onion, garlic, and minced ginger, and sauté until softened and fragrant, about 3-4 minutes. Add the meat pieces and cook until browned on all sides.

Next, make the broth by adding the rinsed rice to the pot with the meat. Pour in the chicken or beef broth and stir to combine. Add the smashed lemongrass and kaffir lime leaves (if using), and stir in the ground turmeric, cumin, coriander, black pepper, soy sauce or fish sauce, salt, and sugar (if using). Bring the mixture to a boil, then reduce the heat to low and simmer uncovered, stirring occasionally, until the rice breaks down and the porridge becomes thick and creamy, about 30-40 minutes.

If you are using coconut milk, stir it in during the last 10 minutes of cooking to add creaminess to the porridge.

Once ready, ladle the Bubur Lambuk into bowls and garnish with fried shallots, chopped fresh cilantro, sliced red chili and lime wedges on the side for extra flavor and spice.

Bubur Lambuk is a flavorful and comforting porridge, perfect for sharing with family and friends. Enjoy it with a variety of garnishes to enhance its rich taste!

Creamy Miso Mushroom Congee

Prep Time	Cooking Time	Serving Size
20 minutes	1 hour	4 servings

Ingredients:

For the Congee:
- 1 cup short-grain rice or jasmine rice
- 6 cups chicken or vegetable broth
- 1 cup mushrooms (such as shiitake, cremini, or a mix), sliced
- 2 tablespoons vegetable oil
- 1 onion, finely chopped
- 4 cloves garlic, minced
- 1 thumb-sized piece of ginger, minced
- 3 tablespoons white miso paste
- 1 cup coconut milk or heavy cream (for creaminess)
- 2 tablespoons soy sauce (adjust to taste)
- 1 teaspoon salt (adjust to taste)
- 1/2 teaspoon ground black pepper

For Garnish:
- Sliced green onions
- Chopped fresh cilantro
- Sesame seeds
- Sliced red chili (optional)
- Fried shallots (optional)
- Pickled vegetables (optional)

Instructions:

Start by rinsing the rice under cold water until the water runs clear to remove excess starch. In a large pot, heat vegetable oil over medium heat, then add the chopped onion, garlic, and ginger. Sauté until the mixture is softened and fragrant, which should take about 3-4 minutes. Next, add the sliced mushrooms and cook until they are softened and beginning to brown, roughly 5-7 minutes.

Add the rinsed rice to the pot with the mushrooms and stir to coat the rice with the oil and aromatics. Pour in the chicken or vegetable broth and bring the mixture to a boil. Reduce the heat to low and let it simmer uncovered, stirring occasionally, until the rice breaks down and the porridge reaches a thick and creamy consistency, about 30-40 minutes.

For added flavor and creaminess, mix the white miso paste with a ladleful of hot broth from the pot in a small bowl until smooth, then stir this mixture back into the pot. Add the coconut milk or heavy cream, soy sauce, salt, and black pepper. Simmer for another 5-10 minutes to meld the flavors and achieve a creamy texture.

Ladle the creamy miso mushroom congee into bowls and garnish with sliced green onions, chopped fresh cilantro, sesame seeds, and sliced red chili if desired. Optionally, serve with fried shallots and pickled vegetables on the side. This congee is a comforting and flavorful dish, rich with the umami depth of miso and the earthy taste of mushrooms. Enjoy it warm with your favorite garnishes!

Borbor Sach Chrouk

Prep Time	**Cooking Time**	**Serving Size**
25 minutes	1 hour	4 servings

Ingredients:

For the Porridge:
- 1 cup jasmine rice (or short-grain rice)
- 6 cups chicken or pork broth (or water)
- 1/2 pound pork tenderloin or pork belly, thinly sliced
- 2 tablespoons vegetable oil
- 1 onion, finely chopped
- 4 cloves garlic, minced
- 1 thumb-sized piece of ginger, minced
- 2-3 stalks lemongrass, smashed
- 2-3 kaffir lime leaves (optional, torn)
- 2 tablespoons fish sauce (adjust to taste)
- 1 teaspoon salt (adjust to taste)
- 1/2 teaspoon ground black pepper

For Garnish:
- Sliced green onions
- Chopped fresh cilantro
- Bean sprouts
- Sliced fresh chili (optional)
- Lime wedges
- Fried shallots (optional)
- Fresh herbs like basil or mint (optional)

Instructions:

To prepare Borbor Sach Chrouk, start by rinsing the rice under cold water until it runs clear to remove excess starch.

For the pork, heat vegetable oil in a large pot over medium heat. Add the chopped onion, garlic, and minced ginger, and sauté until they are softened and fragrant, about 3-4 minutes. Add the sliced pork to the pot and cook until it is lightly browned on all sides, about 5-7 minutes.

To make the broth, add the rinsed rice to the pot with the pork. Pour in the chicken or pork broth (or water) and stir to combine. Add the smashed lemongrass and kaffir lime leaves if using. Bring the mixture to a boil, then reduce the heat to low and simmer uncovered, stirring occasionally, until the rice breaks down and the porridge becomes thick and creamy, about 30-40 minutes.

Once the porridge has thickened, stir in the fish sauce, salt, and black pepper. Adjust the seasoning to taste.

Ladle the Borbor Sach Chrouk into bowls and garnish with sliced green onions, chopped fresh cilantro, and bean sprouts. Top with sliced fresh chili and fried shallots if desired. Serve with lime wedges and additional fresh herbs on the side for extra flavor.

Borbor Sach Chrouk is a satisfying and flavorful rice porridge that combines the savory taste of pork with aromatic spices. Enjoy this comforting dish with your favorite garnishes!

Borbor Sach Moan

Prep Time
25 minutes

Cooking Time
1 hour

Serving Size
4 servings

Ingredients:

For the Porridge:
- 1 cup jasmine rice (or short-grain rice)
- 6 cups chicken broth or water
- 1 pound chicken thighs or drumsticks (bone-in or boneless, as preferred)
- 2 tablespoons vegetable oil
- 1 onion, finely chopped
- 4 cloves garlic, minced
- 1 thumb-sized piece of ginger, minced
- 2-3 stalks lemongrass, smashed
- 2-3 kaffir lime leaves (optional, torn)
- 2 tablespoons fish sauce (adjust to taste)
- 1 teaspoon salt (adjust to taste)
- 1/2 teaspoon ground black pepper

For Garnish:
- Sliced green onions
- Chopped fresh cilantro
- Bean sprouts
- Sliced fresh chili (optional)
- Lime wedges
- Fried shallots (optional)
- Fresh herbs like basil or mint (optional)

Instructions:

To prepare Borbor Sach Moan, start by rinsing the rice under cold water until the water runs clear, which helps remove excess starch.

For the chicken, heat vegetable oil in a large pot over medium heat. Add the chopped onion, garlic, and minced ginger, and sauté until softened and fragrant, about 3-4 minutes. Add the chicken pieces to the pot and cook until lightly browned on all sides, about 5-7 minutes.

To make the broth, add the rinsed rice to the pot with the chicken. Pour in the chicken broth or water, and stir to combine. Add the smashed lemongrass and kaffir lime leaves if using. Bring the mixture to a boil, then reduce the heat to low and simmer uncovered, stirring occasionally, until the rice breaks down and the porridge becomes thick and creamy, about 30-40 minutes.

Once the porridge is thickened, stir in the fish sauce, salt, and black pepper. Adjust the seasoning to taste.

Ladle the Borbor Sach Moan into bowls and garnish with sliced green onions, chopped fresh cilantro, and bean sprouts. Top with sliced fresh chili and fried shallots if desired. Serve with lime wedges and additional fresh herbs on the side for added flavor.

Borbor Sach Moan is a rich and flavorful rice porridge that's both comforting and nutritious. Enjoy the aromatic broth and tender chicken with your favorite garnishes!

Arroz Caldo

Prep Time
20 minutes

Cooking Time
1 hour

Serving Size
4 servings

Ingredients:

- 1 cup jasmine rice (or short-grain rice)
- 6 cups chicken broth
- 2 tablespoons vegetable oil
- 1 onion, finely chopped
- 4 cloves garlic, minced
- 1 thumb-sized piece of ginger, sliced into thin strips
- 1 pound chicken thighs or drumsticks, skinless and bone-in (or boneless, if preferred)
- 1-2 tablespoons fish sauce (adjust to taste)
- 1 teaspoon salt (adjust to taste)
- 1/2 teaspoon ground black pepper
- 2-3 green onions, sliced
- 1 tablespoon soy sauce (optional, for additional flavor)

For Garnish:
- Fried garlic
- Sliced green onions
- Chopped fresh cilantro or parsley
- Hard-boiled eggs, peeled and halved
- Lemon or calamansi wedges
- Crispy fried onions (optional)
- Fish sauce or soy sauce (for additional seasoning)

Instructions:

To prepare Arroz Caldo, start by rinsing the rice under cold water until the water runs clear, which helps remove excess starch.

In a large pot, heat vegetable oil over medium heat. Add the chopped onion and cook until softened, about 3-4 minutes. Then, add the minced garlic and sliced ginger, cooking for another minute until fragrant. Add the chicken pieces to the pot and cook until lightly browned on all sides, about 5-7 minutes.

Next, add the rinsed rice to the pot, stirring to combine with the chicken and aromatics. Pour in the chicken broth and bring the mixture to a boil. Reduce the heat to low and let it simmer uncovered, stirring occasionally, until the rice breaks down and the porridge becomes thick and creamy, about 30-40 minutes.

Stir in the fish sauce, salt, and black pepper, adjusting the seasoning to taste. If you prefer a richer flavor, you can add soy sauce at this point.

To finish, ladle the Arroz Caldo into bowls and garnish with fried garlic, sliced green onions, and chopped fresh cilantro or parsley. Top each serving with halved hard-boiled eggs, and serve with lemon or calamansi wedges on the side for added brightness. For extra flavor, add crispy fried onions and additional fish sauce or soy sauce if desired.

Arroz Caldo is a warm and comforting dish, perfect for any time you need a satisfying meal. Enjoy it with the various garnishes to enhance its flavor and texture!

Made in United States
Troutdale, OR
11/27/2024

25356227R00044